Langenscheidt

Korean

at your Fingertips

Tien Tammada

Langenscheidt

Foreword

Traveling to foreign or to distant lands is a wonderful and exciting thing to do. In fact, it probably features top of the list in worldwide rankings.

However, before every journey to a foreign country, there is a hurdle to be cleared and this hurdle is called "foreign languages". For many, this hurdle seems insurmountable. As a result, they have to give up their life's dream.

What a pity!

You may be planning a week's holiday in Korea to experience the magical countryside or considering moving to live and work in Korea,

Whatever your motivation, don't wait.
Don't let this hurdle stop you from fulfilling your lifelong dreams!
Take courage to embark on this exciting journey to the Korean language

Now!

Once you've made the decision, you'll find that this book provides you with the first helpful steps. You don't need to book a language course and you don't need to worry about complicated grammatical points.

Anyone who has learnt to master a foreign language knows that the essential and really crucial thing about learning a language is actually quite simple: you need to jump in at the deep end. Once you're in the water, everything flows from there.

Jump and don't think twice! You'll learn by doing, not by preparing. The pictures, the selection of important words and useful phrases that you'll find in this book are an important first step. As soon as you come up against the first language hurdle, you can open the book at the appropriate page and find the necessary words and phrases.

If that doesn't work, try pointing to the relevant picture or sentence with your finger. People will know immediately what you mean.
It's really all very easy and convenient. That's why the book is called:

"Korean at your Fingertips".

Content

Useful daily conversations

유익한 일상 대화
[yu-i-khan il-sang de-hwa]

Greeting

인사말
[in-sa-mal]

안녕히 주무셨어요? / 잘 잤어?	**안녕하세요!**	**안녕하세요!**
[an-nyeong-hi ju-mu-syeos-seo-yo / jal jas-seo]	[an-nyeong-ha-se-yo]	[an-nyeong-ha-sey-o]
Good morning!	Good day!	Good evening!

어떻게 지내세요? / 잘 지내요?
[eo-tteoh-ge ji-ne-se-yo / jal ji-ne-yo]

How are you?

네, 잘 지내요. 당신은요?
[ne, jal ji-ne-yo dang-si-neun-yo]

I'm fine, thank you.

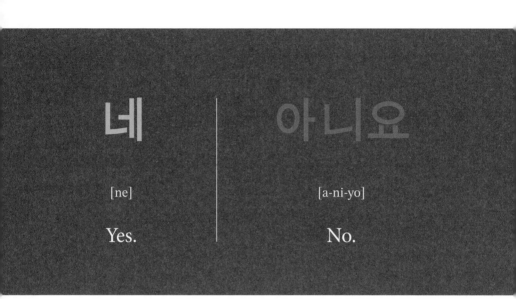

네 | 아니요

[ne] | [a-ni-yo]

Yes. | No.

고마워요. | 정말 고마워요. | 별말씀을요. | 천만에요.

[ko-ma-wo-yo] | [jeong-mal ko-ma-wo-yo] | [byeol-mal-sseu-meu-ryo] | [cheon-ma-ne-yo]

Thanks. | Thank you very much. | You're welcome. | With pleasure.

제 이름은 ... 이에요. / 예요. [je-i-reu-meun ... i-e-yo / ye-yo]	My name is…
당신은 이름이 뭐예요? [dang-si-neun i-reu-mi mwo-ye-yo]	What is your name?
만나서 반가워요. [man-na-seo ban-ga-wo-yo]	Nice to meet you.
저는 미국에서 왔어요. [jeo-neun mi-gug-e-seo was-seo-yo]	I'm from the United States of America.
저는 한국어를 못해요. [jeo-neun han-gu-geo-reul mo-te-yo]	I don't speak Korean.
저는 한국어를 조금 할 수 있어요. [jeo-neun han-gu-geo-reul jo-geum hal su is-seo-yo]	I speak a little Korean.
한국어로 어떻게 말해요? [han-gu-keo-ro eo-tteo-ke mal-he-yo]	How do you say that in Korean?
다시 한 번 말해 줄 수 있어요? [da-si han beon mal-he jul su is-seo-yo]	Could you repeat that, please?
천천히 말해 줄 수 있어요? [cheon-cheon-hi mal-he jul su is-seo-yo]	Could you speak a little more slowly, please?

실례합니다, ...에 어떻게 가나요?

[sil-lye-ham-nida, ... e eo-tteo-ge ga-na-yo]

Excuse me, how can I get to ...?

그게 무슨 뜻이에요? [geu-ge mu-seun tteu-si-e-yo]	What does that mean?
그게 뭐예요? [geu-ge mwo-ye-yo]	What is that?
뭐라고요? [mwo-ra-go-yo]	I beg your pardon? (What did you say?)
실례합니다. [sil-lye-ham-ni-da]	Excuse me.
괜찮아요. [kwen-cha-na-yo]	No problem.
여기가 어디에요? [yeo-gi-ga eo-di-e-yo]	Where am I?
...에 어떻게 가요? [e eo-tteo-ge ga-yo]	How do I get to ...?
여기서 얼마나 멉니까? [yeo-gi-seo eol-ma-na meob-nik-ka]	How far is it from here?
...씨 [ssi]	Mr. ... / Mrs. ... / Miss ...

... 어디에 있어요? [eo-di-e is-seo-yo]	Where is ...?
저는 ... 고 싶어요. [jeo-neun ... go si-peo-yo]	I would like ...
얼마예요? [eol-ma-ye-yo]	How much does it cost?
저는 이게 마음에 들어요. / 저는 이게 좋아요. [jeo-neun ige ma-eume deu-reo-yo/ jeo-neun ige joh-a-yo]	I like this.
저는 이거 별로예요. / 저는 이거 싫어요. [jeo-neun i-geo byeol-lo-yeyo / jeo-neun i-geo si-reo-yo]	I don't like this.
그저 그래요. [keu-jeo geu-re-yo]	So-so.
좋아요. [jo-ayo]	good
아주 좋아요. [a-ju jo-ayo]	very good
대단해요! [te-dan-he-yo]	Great!
완벽해! [wan-byeo-ge]	Perfect!

나빠요. [na-ppa-yo]	bad
아주 나빠요. [a-ju na-ppa-yo]	very bad
많이 [ma-ni]	a lot
조금 [jo-geum]	little
약간 [yak-gan]	some, a bit
잠시만요. [jam-si-man-yo]	Wait a minute, please.
잠깐만요. [jam-ggan-man-yo]	Just a moment, please.
또 봐요! [tto bwa-yo]	See you again!
나중에 봐요! [na-jung-e bwa-yo]	See you later!
내일 봐요! [ne-il bwa-yo]	See you tomorrow!

안녕히 가세요. [an-nyeong-hi ga-seyo]	Good bye! (formal) (When the other goes.)
잘가. [jal-ga]	Bye! (colloquial) (When the other goes.)
안녕히 계세요. [an-nyeong-hi ge-se-yo]	Good bye! (formal) (When you go and the other stays.)
잘있어. [jal-i-sseo]	Bye! (colloquial) (When you go and the other stays.)
누구예요? [nu-gu-ye-yo]	Who?
뭐예요? [mwo-ye-yo]	What?
어디에요? [eo-di-e-yo]	Where?
언제요? [eon-je-yo]	When?
왜요? [we-yo]	Why?
어떻게요? [eo-tteo-ke-yo]	How?
얼마나 많이요? / 몇 개요? [eol-ma-na ma-ni-yo / myeot ge-yo]	How much? / How many?

안녕히 계세요! / 잘 있어!

[an-nyeong-hi ge-se-yo / jal isseo]

Good bye! / Bye!

안녕히 가세요! / 잘 가!

[an-nyeong-hi ga-se-yo / jal ga]

Good bye! / Bye!

At the airport
공항에서 [gong-hang-e-seo]

공항
[gong-hang]

the airport

출입국 관리소가 어디에 있어요?
[chu-lib-guk gwal-li-so-ga
eo-di-e is-seo-yo]

Where is passport control?

비행기 [pi-heng-gi]

실례합니다, 도심에 어떻게 갈 수 있나요?
[sil-le-ham-nida, do-si-me eo-tteo-ke gal su i-na-yo]
Excuse me, how can I get to the city?

기차역이 어디에 있어요?
[gi-cha-yeo-gi eo-di-e-is-seo-yo]
Where is the train station?

출구 →

실례합니다, 출구가 어디에 있어요?
[sil-le-ham-ni-da chul-gu-ga eo-di-e-is-seo-yo]

Excuse me, where is the exit?

the airplane

버스 정류장이 어디에 있어요?
[beo-seu jeong-yu-ja-ngi eo-di-e-is-seo-yo]
Where is the bus stop?

택시를 어디에서 탈 수 있어요?
[tek-si-reul eo-di-e-seo tal su is-seo-yo]
Where can I get a taxi?

관광 안내소가 어디에 있어요?
[kwan-kwang an-ne-so-ga eo-di-e-is-seo-yo]
Where is the tourist information?

도심까지 얼마나 걸려요?
[do-sim-gga-ji eol-mana gyeol-ryeo-yo]
How far is it to the city centre?

저렴한 호텔을 추천해 줄 수 있나요?
[jeo-ryeom-han ho-te-reul chu-cheon-he jul su in-na-yo]
Can you recommend an affordable hotel?

이 주소로 데려다 주세요.
[i ju-so-lo de-lyeo-da ju-se-yo]
Drive me to this address, please.

버스
[beo-seu]
bus

마을버스
[ma-eul-beo-seu]
minibus

운행 비용이 얼마예요?
[un-heng bi-yo-ngi eol-ma-ye-yo]
How much does the ride cost?

신용카드로 계산해도 되나요?
[sin-yong-ka-deu-ro gye-san-he-do dwe-na-yo]
Can I pay by credit card?

언제 내려야 하는지 알려주실 수 있나요?
[eon-je ne-ryeo-ya ha-neun-ji al-ryeo-ju-sil su in-na-yo]
Could you tell me when to get off please?

도와주셔서 정말 감사합니다.
[do-wa-ju-syeo-seo jeong-mal gam-sa-ham-ni-da]
Thank you very much for your help.

택시
[tek-si]

taxi

기차
[ki-cha]

train

지하철
[ji-ha-cheol]

subway

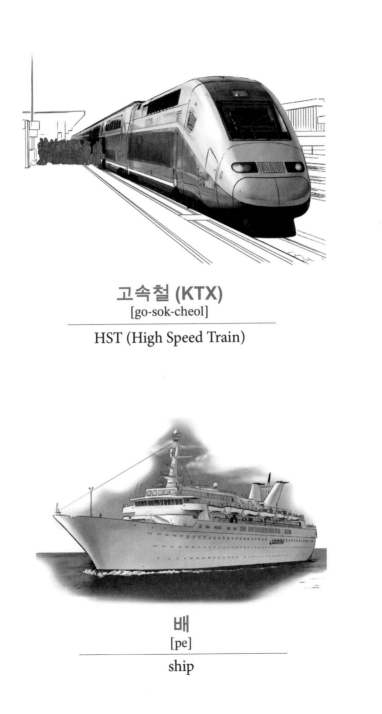

고속철 (KTX)
[go-sok-cheol]

HST (High Speed Train)

배
[pe]

ship

Accommodation

숙소 [suk-so]

빈 방이 있나요?

[bin-ba-ngi in-na-yo]

Is there any room available?

방을 볼 수 있나요?

[bang-eul bol su in-na-yo]

May I see the room, please?

얼마예요?

[eol-ma-ye-yo]

How much is it?

아침식사가 포함되어 있나요?

[a-chim-sik-sa-ga po-ham-dwe-eo in-na-yo]

Is breakfast included?

방을 ... 이름으로 예약했어요.

[bang-eul ... i-reu-meu-ro ye-yak-he-sseo-yo]

I have booked (a room) in the name of ...

여기 제 여권이에요.
[yeo-gi je yeo-gwo-ni-e-yo]

Here is my passport.

와이파이가 있나요?
[wa-i-pa-i-ga in-na-yo]

Do you have wireless Internet?

금고가 있나요?
[geum-go-ga in-na-yo]

Do you have a safe?

몇 시에 체크아웃해야 해요?
[myeot-si-e che-keu-a-u-the-ya he-yo]

When do I have to check out?

접수 창구가 항상 열려 있나요?
[jeob-su chang-gu-ga hang-sang
yeol-lyeo in-na-yo]

Is reception open all the time?

... 방을 주세요.

[bang-eul ju-seyo]

I would like a room for ...

한 명
[han myeong]
one person.

두 명
[du myeong]
two people.

가족
[ga-jok]
a family.

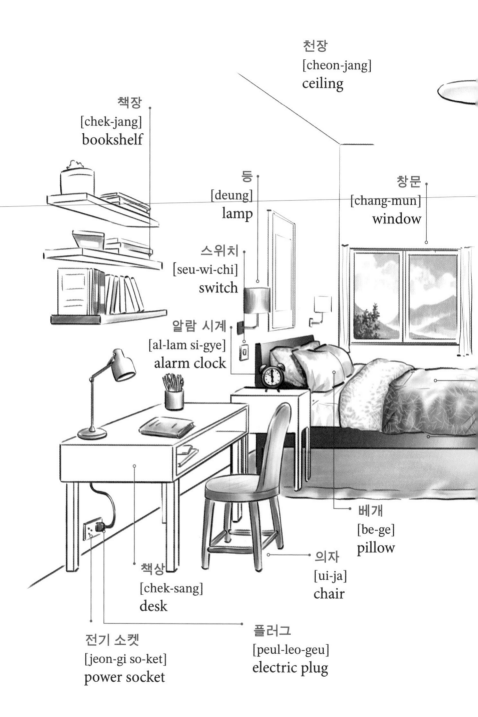

천장
[cheon-jang]
ceiling

책장
[chek-jang]
bookshelf

등
[deung]
lamp

창문
[chang-mun]
window

스위치
[seu-wi-chi]
switch

알람 시계
[al-lam si-gye]
alarm clock

베개
[be-ge]
pillow

책상
[chek-sang]
desk

의자
[ui-ja]
chair

전기 소켓
[jeon-gi so-ket]
power socket

플러그
[peul-leo-geu]
electric plug

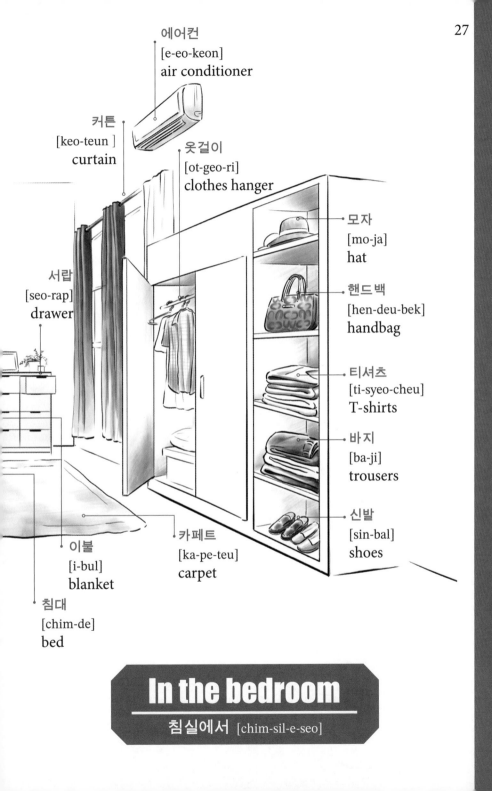

에어컨
[e-eo-keon]
air conditioner

커튼
[keo-teun]
curtain

옷걸이
[ot-geo-ri]
clothes hanger

서랍
[seo-rap]
drawer

모자
[mo-ja]
hat

핸드백
[hen-deu-bek]
handbag

티셔츠
[ti-syeo-cheu]
T-shirts

바지
[ba-ji]
trousers

신발
[sin-bal]
shoes

이불
[i-bul]
blanket

카페트
[ka-pe-teu]
carpet

침대
[chim-de]
bed

In the bedroom
침실에서 [chim-sil-e-seo]

In the bathroom

욕실에서 [yok-sil-e-seo]

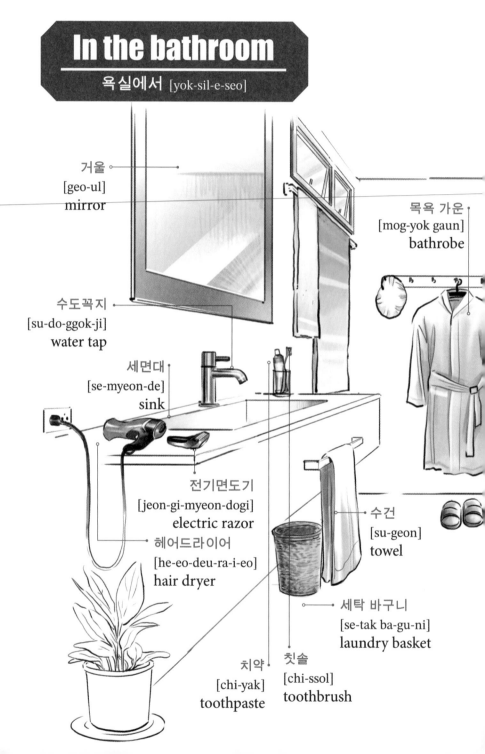

거울
[geo-ul]
mirror

목욕 가운
[mog-yok gaun]
bathrobe

수도꼭지
[su-do-ggok-ji]
water tap

세면대
[se-myeon-de]
sink

전기면도기
[jeon-gi-myeon-dogi]
electric razor

헤어드라이어
[he-eo-deu-ra-i-eo]
hair dryer

수건
[su-geon]
towel

세탁 바구니
[se-tak ba-gu-ni]
laundry basket

치약
[chi-yak]
toothpaste

칫솔
[chi-ssol]
toothbrush

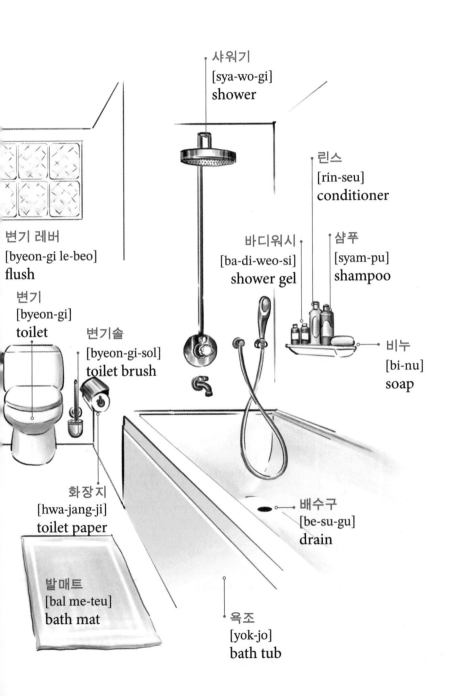

샤워기
[sya-wo-gi]
shower

린스
[rin-seu]
conditioner

바디워시
[ba-di-weo-si]
shower gel

샴푸
[syam-pu]
shampoo

변기 레버
[byeon-gi le-beo]
flush

변기
[byeon-gi]
toilet

변기솔
[byeon-gi-sol]
toilet brush

비누
[bi-nu]
soap

화장지
[hwa-jang-ji]
toilet paper

배수구
[be-su-gu]
drain

발매트
[bal me-teu]
bath mat

욕조
[yok-jo]
bath tub

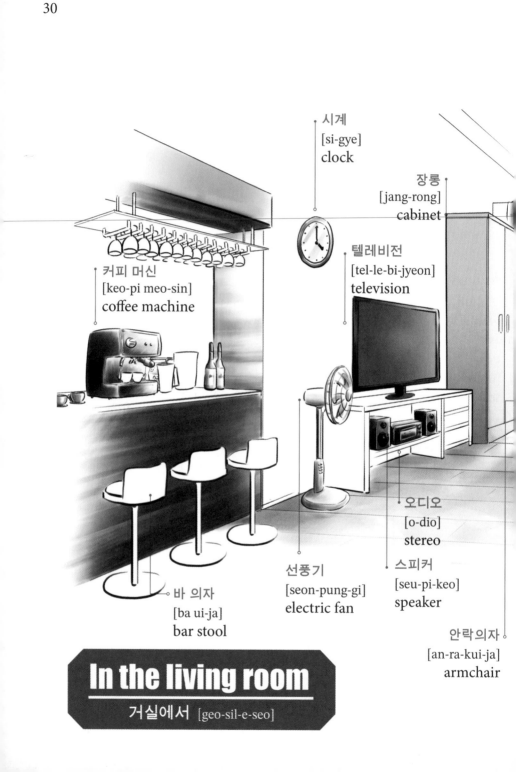

시계
[si-gye]
clock

장롱
[jang-rong]
cabinet

커피 머신
[keo-pi meo-sin]
coffee machine

텔레비전
[tel-le-bi-jyeon]
television

오디오
[o-dio]
stereo

바 의자
[ba ui-ja]
bar stool

선풍기
[seon-pung-gi]
electric fan

스피커
[seu-pi-keo]
speaker

안락의자
[an-ra-kui-ja]
armchair

In the living room
거실에서 [geo-sil-e-seo]

등
[deung]
lamp

피아노
[pi-a-no]
piano

그림
[geu-rim]
picture

책
[chek]
books

바이올린
[ba-i-ol-lin]
violin

테이블
[te-i-beul]
table

꽃병
[ggot-byeong]
vase

꽃
[ggot]
flowers

리모컨
[ri-mo-keon]
remote control

소파
[so-pa]
sofa

전화기
[jeon-hwa-gi]
telephone

프라이팬
[peu-ra-i-pen]
frying pan

병
[byeong]
bottle

컵
[keop]
cup

와인글라스
[wa-in-geul-la-seu]
wine glass

젓가락
jeot-ga-rak
chopsticks

접시
[jeop-si]
plate

숟가락
[sut-ga-rak]
spoon

포크
[po-keu]
fork

거품기
[geo-pum-gi]
whisk

도마
[do-ma]
chopping board

수도꼭지
[sudo-ggok-ji]
faucet

전자레인지
[jeon-ja-re-in-ji]
microwave

In the kitchen

부엌에서 [bu-eok-e-seo]

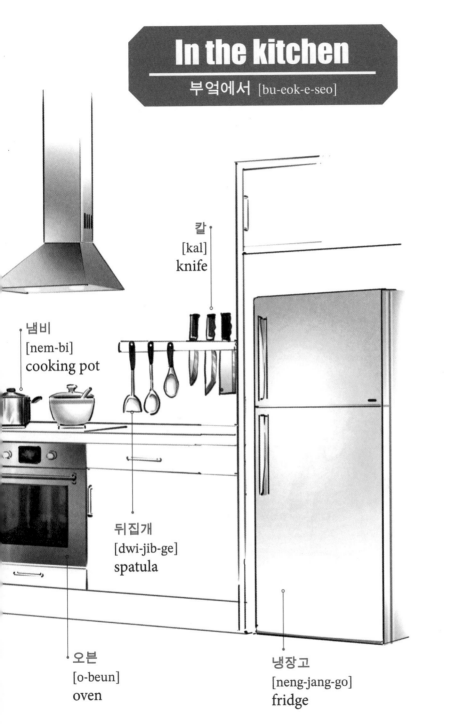

칼
[kal]
knife

냄비
[nem-bi]
cooking pot

뒤집개
[dwi-jib-ge]
spatula

오븐
[o-beun]
oven

냉장고
[neng-jang-go]
fridge

Excursions (in the city and in the countryside)

여행(도시와 시골에서)
[yeo-heng(do-si-wa si-go-re-seo)]

이 근처에 관광 명소가 있나요?

[i geun-cheo-e gwan-gwang myeong-so-ga in-na-yo]

Are there any tourist attractions in this area?

어디에서 전통 지방음식을 맛볼 수 있나요?

[eo-di-e-seo jeon-tong ji-bang-eum-si-keul mat-bol su in-na-yo]

Where can I taste the traditional local food?

Excursions by train

기차여행 [gi-cha-yeo-heng]

기차역이 어디에 있어요?
[gi-cha-yeo-ki eo-di-e -is-seo-yo]

Where is the train station?

승차권 자동판매기는
어디에 있어요?
[seung-cha-gwon ja-dong-pan-me-gi-neun eo-di-e-is-seo-yo]

Where is the ticket vending machine?

매표소가 어디에 있어요?
[me-pyo-soga eo-di-e-is-seo-yo]

Where is the ticket office?

표는 얼마인가요?
[pyo-neun eol-ma-in-ga-yo]

How much does the ticket cost?

특실 표 주세요.
[teug-sil pyo ju-se-yo]

One first-class ticket, please.

일반실 표 주세요.
[il-ban-sil pyo ju-se-yo]

One second-class ticket, please.

편도 표 주세요.
[pyeon-do pyo ju-se-yo]

A one-way ticket, please

| 왕복 표 주세요. | A round-trip ticket, please. |
| [wang-bok pyo ju-se-yo] | |

| 좌석을 예약하고 싶어요. | I would like to reserve a seat, |
| [jwa-seo-geul yeo-yak-ha-go si-peo-yo] | please. |

| 기차는 몇 시에 출발해요? | What time does the train leave? |
| [gi-cha-neun myeot-si-e chul-bal-he-yo] | |

열차를 몇 번 갈아타야 하나요?	How many times do I have to
[yeol-cha-reul myeot beon ga-ra-ta-ya	change trains?
ha-na-yo]	

| 다음 역의 이름이 뭐예요? | What is the next station? |
| [da-eum yeo-keui i-reu-mi mwo-ye-yo] | |

언제 내려야 하는지 알려주세요.	Please tell me when I have to
[eon-je ne-ryeo-ya ha-neun-ji	get off.
al-lyeo-ju-se-yo]	

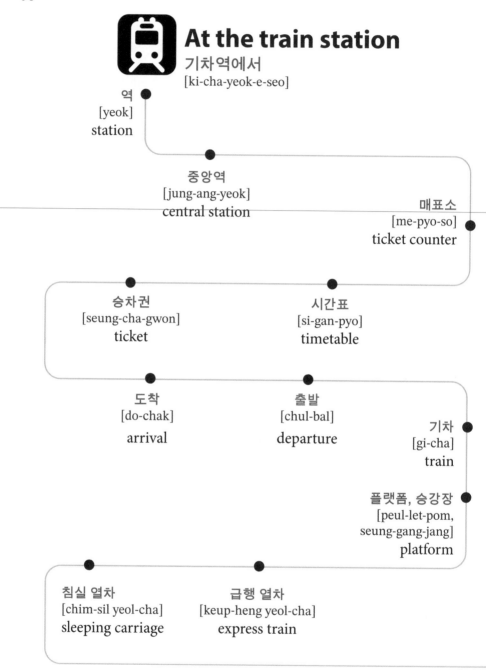

At the train station
기차역에서
[ki-cha-yeok-e-seo]

역
[yeok]
station

중앙역
[jung-ang-yeok]
central station

매표소
[me-pyo-so]
ticket counter

승차권
[seung-cha-gwon]
ticket

시간표
[si-gan-pyo]
timetable

도착
[do-chak]
arrival

출발
[chul-bal]
departure

기차
[gi-cha]
train

플랫폼, 승강장
[peul-let-pom,
seung-gang-jang]
platform

침실 열차
[chim-sil yeol-cha]
sleeping carriage

급행 열차
[keup-heng yeol-cha]
express train

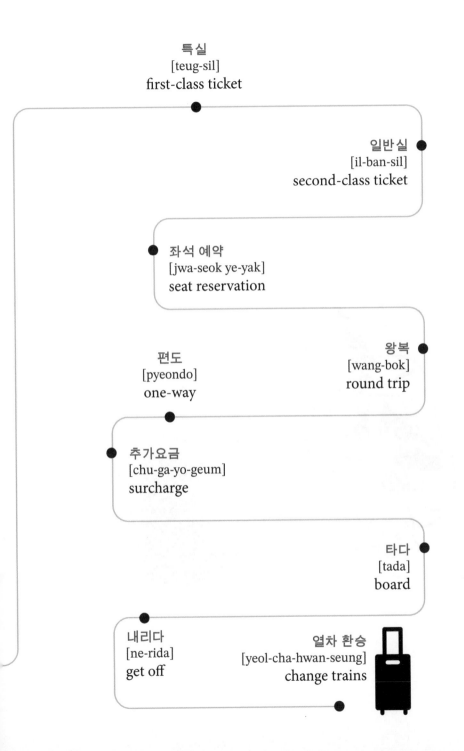

특실
[teug-sil]
first-class ticket

일반실
[il-ban-sil]
second-class ticket

좌석 예약
[jwa-seok ye-yak]
seat reservation

편도
[pyeondo]
one-way

왕복
[wang-bok]
round trip

추가요금
[chu-ga-yo-geum]
surcharge

타다
[tada]
board

내리다
[ne-rida]
get off

열차 환승
[yeol-cha-hwan-seung]
change trains

기차/버스 몇 시에 출발해요?

[ki-cha/peo-seu myeot si-e chul-ba-re-yo]

What time does the train / the bus leave?

실례합니다,
승차권 구매하는 것 좀 도와주실 수 있나요?

[sil-lye-ham-ni-da,
seung-cha-gwan gu-me-ha-neun geot jom do-wa-ju-sil su in-na-yo]

Excuse me,
can you help me buy a ticket please?

저는...에 가고 싶어요.

[jeo-neun ...e ga-go si-peo-yo]

I want to go to ...

Travel by bus and subway

버스와 지하절로 하는 여행
[peo-seu-wa-ji-ha-jeol-lo ha-neun-yeo-heng]

버스 [beo-seu]	bus
버스 정류장 [beo-seu jeong-ryu-jang]	bus stop
지하철 [ji-ha-cheol]	subway

지하철역이 어디에 있어요?
[ji-ha-cheol-yeo-ki-eo-di-e-is-seo-yo]
Where is the subway station?

지하철역 [ji-ha-cheol-yeok]	subway station
승차권 [seung-cha-gwon]	ticket
검표원 [geom-pyo-won]	ticket inspector
벌금 [beol-geum]	fine / penalty

... 어디에 있어요?

[eo-di-e-is-seo-yo]

Where is ...?

버스 정류장이 어디에 있어요?

[beo-seu jeong-ryu-jangi eo-di-e- is-seo-yo]

Where is the bus stop?

신호등

[sin-ho-deung]

traffic light

오토바이

[o-to-ba-i]

motocycle

자전거

[ja-jeon-geo]

bicycle

자동차

[ja-dong-cha]

car

Travelling on your own by car, motocycle, bicycle and on foot

자동차, 오토바이, 자전거, 혹은 도보로 하는 여행
[ja-dong-cha, o-to-ba-i, ja-jeon-geo, ho-geun doboro ha-neun yeo-heng]

거리 [geo-ri]	street
교차로 [gyo-cha-ro]	intersection
직진하다 [jik-jin-ha-da]	go straight on
우회전 [wu-hoe-jeon]	turn right
좌회전 [jwa-hoe-jeon]	turn left
여기 [yeo-gi]	here
저기 [jeo-gi]	over there
가깝다 [ka-ggap-da]	near
멀다 [meol-da]	far
보험 [bo-heom]	insurance
주유소가 어디에요? [ju-yu-so-ga eo-di-eyo]	Where is the gas station?
어떤 기름을 넣어야 해요? [eo-tteon gi-reu-meul neo-eo-ya-he-yo]	What kind of gas should I put in?

Art and leisure time activities

예술 및 레저 활동 [ye-sul mit re-jeo hwal-dong]

극장
[geuk-jang]
the theatre

오페라 극장
[o-pe-ra geuk-jang]
the opera house

영화관
[yeong-hwa-gwan]
the cinema

미술관
[mi-sul-gwan]
the art gallery

박물관
[bak-mul-gwan]
the museum

실내 수영장
[sil-le su-yeong-jang]
the indoor swimming pool

야외 수영장
[ya-oe su-yeong-jang]
the outdoor swimming pool

사우나, 목욕탕
[sa-u-na / mo-kyok-tang]
the sauna

공원
[gong-won]
the city park

헬스클럽
[hel-seu-keul-leob]
the gym

Tourist attractions

관광 명소 [gwan-gwang myeong-so]

불국사
[bul-guk-sa]
Bulguksa Temple / (Gyeongju)

감천문화마을
[kam-cheon-mun-hwa-ma-eul]
Gamcheon Culture Village (Busan)

광화문
[gwang-hwa-mun]
Gwanghwamun (Seoul)

후원
[hu-won]
Huwon Secret Garden (Seoul)

화성
[hwa-seong]
Hwaseong Fortress (Suwon)

남이섬
[na-mi-seom]
Namiseom Island (Chuncheon)

포천아트밸리
[po-cheo-na-teu-bel-li]
Pocheon Art Valley (Pocheon)

설악산 국립공원
[seo-rak-san gung-rip-gong-won]
Seoraksan National Park (Sokcho)

Tourist attractions

관광 명소 [gwan-gwang myeong-so]

제주도
[je-ju-do]
Jeju Island

부산
[bu-san]
Busan

경복궁
[gyeong-bok-gung]
Gyeongbok Palace (Seoul)

강화도
[kang-hwa-do]
Ganghwado Island

전주한옥마을
[jeon-ju-ha-nok-ma-eul]
Jeonju hanok Village (Jeonju)

진도
[jindo]
Jindo

보령머드축제
[bo-ryeong-meo-deu-chuk-je]
Boryeong Mud Festival (Boryeong)

Food

Bakery

빵집 [ppang-jib]

호두과자
[ho-du-gwa-ja]

walnut cookies

황남빵
[hwang-nam-ppang]

Hwangnam-bread

소라 빵
[so-ra ppang]

Sora-bread

모찌 빵
[mo-jji ppang]

Mochi-bread

계란 빵
[kye-lan ppang]

egg bread

빵
[ppang]

bread

단팥 빵
[tan-pat ppang]

red bean bread

소보로 빵
[so-bo-ro ppang]

soboro bread

양고기
[yang-go-gi]
lamb

At the butchers

정육점에서 [jeo-ngyuk-jeo-me-seo]

소고기
[so-go-gi]
beef

오리고기
[o-ri-go-gi]
duck

돼지고기
[dwe-ji-go-gi]
pork

닭고기
[dak-go-gi]
chicken

At the fishmonger

생선 가게에서 [seng-seon ka-ge-e-seo]

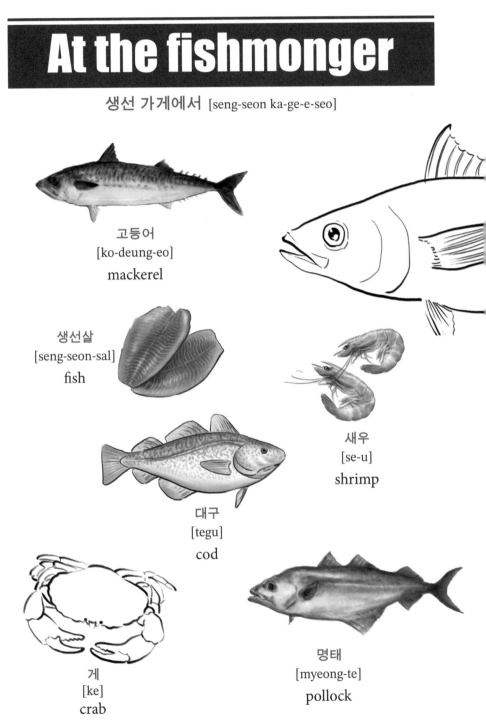

고등어
[ko-deung-eo]
mackerel

생선살
[seng-seon-sal]
fish

새우
[se-u]
shrimp

대구
[tegu]
cod

게
[ke]
crab

명태
[myeong-te]
pollock

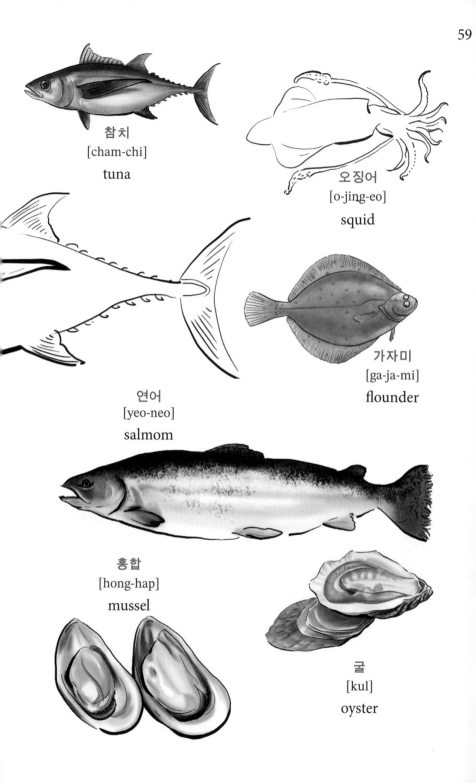

참치
[cham-chi]
tuna

오징어
[o-jing-eo]
squid

가자미
[ga-ja-mi]
flounder

연어
[yeo-neo]
salmom

홍합
[hong-hap]
mussel

굴
[kul]
oyster

1

2

3

4

5

6

7

8

9

In the vegetable shop

야채 가게에서 [ya-che ka-ge-e-seo]

1. 가지 [gaji]
eggplant

2. 오이 [o-i]
cucumber

3. 브로콜리 [beu-ro-kol-li]
broccoli

4. 배추 [pe-chu]
chinese cabbage

5. 무 [mu]
radish

6. 완두콩 [wan-du-kong]
pea

7. 콜리플라워 [kolli-peul-lawo]
cauliflower

8. 당근 [dang-geun]
carrot

9. 고추 [ko-chu]
chili

1. 생강 [seng-gang]
ginger

2. 상추 [sang-chu]
lettuce

3. 호박 [ho-bak]
pumpkin

4. 아몬드 [a-mon-deu]
almond

5. 땅콩 [ttang-kong]
peanut

6. 밤 (열매) [bam (yeol-me)]
chestnut (fruit)

7. 마늘 [ma-neul]
garlic

8. 버섯 [beo-seot]
mushroom

9. 감자 [kam-ja]
potato

10. 옥수수 [ok-su-su]
corn

11. 호두 [ho-du]
walnut

1

2

3

4

5

6

7

8

9

10

1. 비트 [bi-teu]
beetroot

2. 피망 [pi-mang]
sweet pepper

3. 양파 [yang-pa]
onion

4. 양배추 [yang-be-chu]
white cabbage

5. 적양배추 [jeok-yang-be-chu]
red cabbage

6. 아스파라거스 [a-seu-pa-ra-geo-seu]
asparagus

7. 토마토 [to-ma-to]
tomato

8. 애호박 [e-ho-bak]
courgette

9. 셀러리 [sel-leo-ri]
celery

10. 시금치 [si-geum-chi]
spinach

사과 [sa-gwa] apple	**풋사과** [put-sa-gwa] green apple	**배** [pe] pear
체리 [che-ri] cherry	**자두** [ja-du] plum	**올리브** [ol-li-beu] olive
코코넛 [ko-ko-neot] coconut	**딸기** [ttal-gi] strawberry	**파인애플** [pa-i-ne-peul] pineapple

석류	참외	산딸기
[seok-ryu]	[cham-oe]	[san-ttal-gi]
pomegranate	Korean melon	raspberry

In the fruit shop

과일 가게에서 [kwa-il ka-ge-e-seo]

감	블루베리	레몬
[gam]	[beul-lu-be-ri]	[re-mon]
persimmon	blueberry	Korean lemon

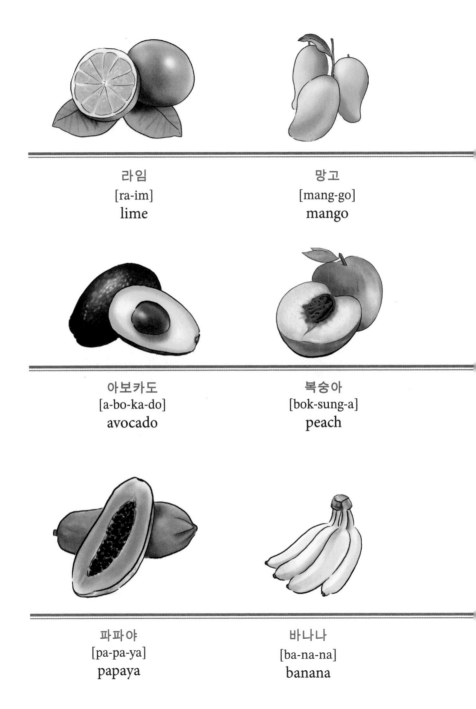

라임
[ra-im]
lime

망고
[mang-go]
mango

아보카도
[a-bo-ka-do]
avocado

복숭아
[bok-sung-a]
peach

파파야
[pa-pa-ya]
papaya

바나나
[ba-na-na]
banana

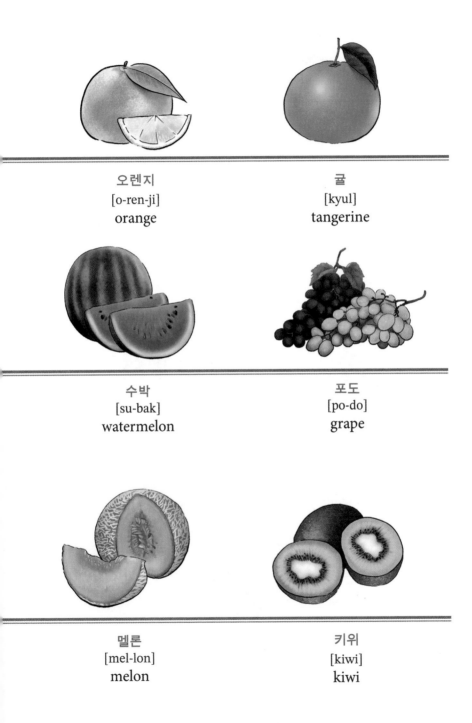

오렌지
[o-ren-ji]
orange

굴
[kyul]
tangerine

수박
[su-bak]
watermelon

포도
[po-do]
grape

멜론
[mel-lon]
melon

키위
[kiwi]
kiwi

Beverages

마실거리 [ma-sil-geo-ri]

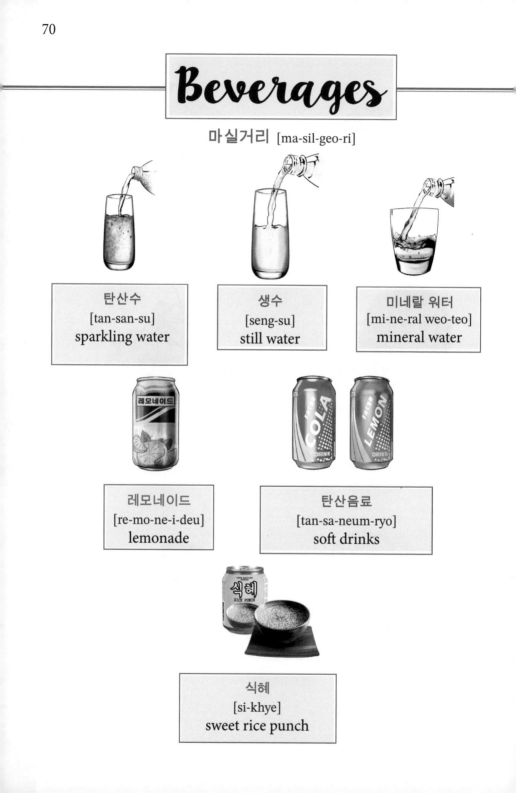

탄산수
[tan-san-su]
sparkling water

생수
[seng-su]
still water

미네랄 워터
[mi-ne-ral weo-teo]
mineral water

레모네이드
[re-mo-ne-i-deu]
lemonade

탄산음료
[tan-sa-neum-ryo]
soft drinks

식혜
[si-khye]
sweet rice punch

당근 주스
[tang-geun ju-seu]
carrot juice

파인애플 주스
[pa-i-ne-peul ju-seu]
pineapple juice

사과 주스
[sa-gwa ju-seu]
apple juice

토마토 주스
[to-ma-to ju-seu]
tomato juice

오렌지 주스
[o-ren-ji ju-seu]
orange juice

포도 주스
[po-do ju-seu]
grape juice

At the bar

바에서 [ba-e-seo]

맥주

[mek-ju]

beer

소주

[so-ju]

soju

청주

[cheong-ju]

cheongju

인삼주

[in-sam-ju]

ginseng liquor

적포도주

jeok-po-do-ju

red wine

백포도주

[bek-po-do-ju]

white wine

로제

[ro-je]

rosé wine

막걸리

[mak-ggeol-li]

rice wine

매실주

[me-sil-ju]

plum wine

안동소주

[an-dong-so-ju]

Andong soju

복분자주

[bok-bun-ja-ju]

black raspberry wine

나쁜와인을

마시기에는

너무 짧은 인생

[nap-peun wa-in-eul ma-si-gi-e-neun neo-mu jjal-beun in-seng]

Life is too short to drink bad wine.

Johann Wolfgang von Goethe

에스프레소
[es-peu-re-so]
Espresso

에스프레소 마키아토
[es-peu-re-so ma-ki-a-tto]
Espresso Macchiato

아메리카노
[a-me-ri-ka-no]
Americano

아포가토
[a-po-ga-to]
Cafe Affogato

At the coffee shop

카페숍에서 [ka-pe-syob-e-seo]

에스프레소 [es-peu-re-so]

espresso

에스프레소 마키아토 [es-peu-re-so ma-ki-a-tto]

double espresso with milk foam

아메리카노 [amerikano]

Americano

아포가토 [a-po-ga-to]

espresso with icecrem

카페라떼 [ka-pe-ra-tte]
Cafe Latte

우유 거품
에스프레소
뜨거운 우유

카푸치노 [ka-pu-chi-no]
Cappuccino

우유 거품
에스프레소
뜨거운 우유

카페모카 [ka-pe-mo-ka]
Mocha

휘핑크림
뜨거운 우유
초콜릿 시럽
에스프레소

핫초코 [hat-cho-ko]
Hot chocolate

핫밀크 [hat-mil-keu]
Hot milk

카페라떼 [ka-pe-ra-tte]
milk coffee
카푸치노 [ka-pu-chi-no]
cappuccino
카페모카 [ka-pe-mo-ka]
espresso with chocolate syrup
핫초코 [hat-cho-ko]
hot chocolate
핫밀크 [hat-mil-keu]
hot milk

1

2

3

4

5

6

Tee
차 [cha]

7

9

10

8

11

12

1. 떡차 [tteok-cha]
rice cake tea

2. 도화차 [do-hwa-cha]
peach blossom tea

3. 국화차 [guk-hwa-cha]
chrysanthemum tea

4. 홍차 [hong-cha]
red tea

5. 황산차 [hwang-san-cha]
rosebay tea

6. 인삼차 [in-sam-cha]
ginseng tea

7. 메밀차 [me-mil-cha]
buckwheat tea

8. 민들레차 [min-deul-le-cha]
dandelion tea

9. 오미자차 [o-mi-ja-cha]
schisandra tea

10. 생강차 [seng-gang-cha]
ginger tea

11. 녹차 [nok-cha]
green tea

12. 연꽃차 [yeon-ggot-cha]
lotus tea

여기요, 주문할게요.

[yeo-gi-yo, ju-mun-hal-ge-yo]

Excuse me, I would like to order, please.

음식을 추천해 주실 수 있나요?

[eum-sik-eul chu-cheon-he ju-sil su in-na-yo]

What would you recommend?

In the restaurant

식당에서 [sik-dang-e-seo]

식당 [sik-dang] restaurant

메뉴 [me-nyu] menu

두 사람 자리가 있나요?
[tu sa-ram ja-ri-ga in-na-yo]

Do you have a table for two?

오늘의 특별 요리는 뭐예요?
[o-neul-ui teuk-byeol yo-ri-neun
mwo-ye-yo]

What is today's special?

음식을 추천해 주실 수 있나요?
[eum-si-keul chu-cheon-he ju-sil
su in-na-yo]

What would you recommend?

...을(를) 주문할게요.
[eul(reul) ju-mun-hal-ge-yo]

I would like...

잘 먹겠습니다.
[jal meok-get-seum-ni-da]

Thank you for this food.
(Said before eating.)

잘 먹었습니다.
[jal meo-keot-seum-nida]

I really enjoyed the meal.
(Said after the meal.)

후추
[hu-chu]
pepper

소금
[so-geum]
salt

Seasonings

양념 [yang-nyeom]

고춧가루
[go-chut-ga-ru]
chili powder

고추장
[go-chu-jang]
chili paste

참기름
[cham-gi-reum]
sesame oil

겨자
[kyeo-ja]
mustard

토마토 소스
[to-ma-to so-seu]
ketchup

마요네즈
[ma-yo-ne-jeu]
mayonnaise

설탕
[seol-tang]
sugar

쌈장
[ssam-jang]
samjang sauce

식초
[sik-cho]
vinegar

파르메산 치즈
[pa-reu-me-san chi-jeu]
parmesan cheese

간장
[gan-jang]
soy sauce

식사	[sik-sa]	meal
아침식사	[a-chim-sik-sa]	breakfast
점심식사	[jeom-sim-sik-sa]	lunch
저녁식사	[jeon-yeok-sik-sa]	dinner

맛있게 드세요!

[ma-sig-ke deu-se-yo]

Enjoy your meal!

계산서 좀 주세요.

[kye-san-seo jom ju-seyo]

May I have the bill, please?

음식이 아주 맛있었어요!
[eum-siki a-ju ma-sis-seo-yo]

The food was very good!

맛있어요!
[ma-sis-seo-yo]

Delicious!

거스름돈은 괜찮습니다.
[geo-seu-reum-do-neun
kwean-chan-seum-ni-da]

Keep the change.

팁
[tɪp]

tip

꿀
[ggul]
honey

버터
[beo-teo]
butter

딸기잼
[ttal-gi-jem]
strawberry jam

뮤즐리
[myu-jeul-li]
cereal

오렌지 마멀레이드
[o-ren-ji ma-meol-le-i-deu]
orange marmalade

요거트
[yo-geo-teu]
yogurt

삶은 달걀
[sal-meun dal-gya]
soft-boiled egg

스크램블드에그
[seu-keu-rem-beul-deu e-geu]
scrambled eggs

한국의서양식아침식사
[han-gu-gui-seo-yang-sik-a-chim-sik-sa]
Western breakfast in Korean

Breakfast

아침식사 [a-chim-sik-sa]

한국의 전통적인 아침식사
[han-gu-gui jeon-tong-jeo-gin a-chim-sik-sa]
Korean traditional breakfast

Typical Korean food
대표적인 한국 음식 [te-pyo-jeo-gin han-gu-geum-sik]

비빔밥
[bi-bim-bap]
bibimbap

불고기
[bul-go-gi]
bulgogi

순두부찌개
[sun-du-bu-jji-ge]
tofu stew

잡채
[jap-che]
stir-fried glass noodles

김치찌개
[gim-chi-jji-ge]
kimchi soup

된장찌개
[doen-jang-jji-ge]
soybean paste stew

제육볶음
[je-yuk-bo-ggeum]
spicy stir-fried pork

삼계탕
[sam-gye-tang]
ginseng chicken soup

냉면
[neng-myeon]
cold buckwheat noodles

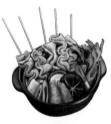

어묵탕
[eo-muk-tang]
fishcake soup

떡볶이
[tteok-bo-ggi]
spicy rice cake

김밥
[gim-bap]
seaweed rice roll

해물파전
[he-mul-pa-jeon]
seafood and green onion pancake

Dessert

디저트 [di-jeo-teu]

---

1. 부꾸미 [bu-ggu-mi]

• • •

2. 다식 [da-sik]

• • •

3. 붕어빵 [bung-eo-ppang]

• • •

4. 빙수 [bing-su]

• • •

5. 호떡 [hot-teok]

• • •

6. 과편 [gwa-pyeon]

• • •

7. 만두과 [man-du-gwa]

• • •

8. 송편 [song-pyeon]

• • •

9. 약과 [yak-gwa]

• • •

10. 약식 [yak-sik]

Places to shop

쇼핑 [syo-ping]

신세계 백화점
[sin-se-gye bek-hwa-jeom]
Shinsegae department store

현대 백화점
[hyeon-de bek-hwa-jeom]
Hyundai department store

롯데 백화점
[lotte bek-hwa-jeon]
Lotte department store

갤러리아 백화점
[kel-leo-ri-a bek-hwa-jeom]
Galeria department store

백화점

[bek-hwa-jeom]
department store

쇼핑센터

[syo-ping-sen-teo]
shopping center

가게

[ka-ge]
shop

수퍼마켓

[su-peo-ma-ket]
supermarket

시장

[si-jang]
market

Everything your heart desires

당신의 마음이 원하는 모든 것
[dang-si-nui ma-eum-i won-ha-neun mo-deun geot]

화장품 가게
[hwa-jang-pum-ka-ge]
cosmetic shop

미용실
[mi-yong-sil]
hair salon

보석 가게
[bo-seok-ka-ge]
jewellery shop

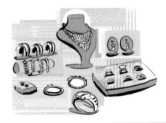

꽃 가게
[ggot-ka-g-e]
flower shop

옷가게
[ot-ka-ge]
fashion boutique

신발 가게
[sin-bal-ka-ge]
shoe shop

기념품 가게
[ki-nyeom-pum-ka-ge]
souvenir shop

골동품 가게
[kol-dong-pum ka-ge]
antique shop

나는 ... 하고 싶다.
[na-neun ... ha-go sip-da]

I would like...

셔츠 한 벌
[syeo-cheu han beol]

a shirt.

바지 한 벌
[baji han beol]

a pair of trousers.

신발 한 켤레
[sin-bal han kyeol-le]

a pair of shoes.

양말 한 켤레
[yang-mal han kyeol-le]

a pair of socks.

블라우스 두 벌
[beul-la-u-seu du beol]

two blouses.

재킷 세 벌
[je-kit se beol]

three jackets.

치마 네 벌
[chi-ma ne beol]

four skirts.

코트 다섯 벌
[ko-teu ta-seot beol]

five coats.

이거 얼마예요?
[i-geo eol-ma-ye-yo]

How much does it cost?

... 원입니다.
[won-im-ni-da]

It costs ... Won.

너무 비싸네요.
[neo-mu bi-ssa-ne-yo]

That is very expensive.

가격을 좀 깎아주실 수 있나요?
[ka-gyeo-geul jom gga-gga-ju-sil
su in-na-yo]

Can you give me discount?

굉장히 저렴하네요.
[koeng-jang-hi jeo-ryeom-ha-ne-yo]

That is very cheap.

고마워요, 충분합니다.
[ko-ma-wo-yo chung-bun-ham-ni-da.]

No more, thanks.

가격이 적당하네요.
[ka-gyeo-gi jeok-dang-ha-ne-yo]

The price is reasonable.

너무 짧아요. / 너무 길어요.
[neo-mu jjal-pa-yo. / neo-mu gi-reo-yo]

It's too short / too long.

너무 커요. / 너무 타이트해요.
[neo-mu keo-yo. /
neo-mu ta-i-teu-he-yo]

It's too loose / too tight.

이 옷을 입어 봐도 될까요?

[i-o-seul i-beo pwa-do dwel-gga-yo]

May I try it on?

피팅 룸은 어디에 있어요?

[pi-ting ru-meun eo-di-e-is-seo-yo]

Where is the fitting room?

특별할인

[teuk-byeo-ra-rin]

Special discount

세일

[se-il]

sale

프로모션

[peu-ro-mo-syeon]

promotion

할인

[ha-rin]

discount

Colors

색깔 [sek-ggal]

흰색
[huin-sek]
white

검정색
[geom-jeong-sek]
black

주황색
[ju-hwang-sek]
orange

갈색
[gal-sek]
brown

회색
[hoe-sek]
grey

하늘색
[ha-neul-sek]
light blue

밝은 ...
[bal-keun]
light

어두운 ...
[eo-du-un]
dark

빨간색
[ppal-gan-sek]
red

분홍색
[pun-hong-sek]
pink

노란색
[no-ran-sek]
yellow

녹색
[nok-sek]
green

파란색
[pa-ran-sek]
dark blue

보라색
[po-ra-sek]
purple

Numbers

숫자 [sut-ja]

Sino-Korean Numbers

0	영	[yeong]	26	이십육	[i-sib-yuk]
1	일	[il]	27	이십칠	[i-sib-chil]
2	이	[i]	28	이십팔	[i-sib--pal]
3	삼	[sam]	29	이십구	[i-sib-gu]
4	사	[sa]	30	삼십	[sam-sib]
5	오	[o]	40	사십	[sa-sib]
6	육	[yuk]	50	오십	[o-sib]
7	칠	[chil]	60	육십	[yuk-sib]
8	팔	[pal]	70	칠십	[chil-sib]
9	구	[gu]	80	팔십	[pal-sib]
10	십	[sib]	90	구십	[gu-sib]
11	십일	[sib-il]	100	백	[pek]
12	십이	[sib-i]	101	백일	[pe-kil]
13	십삼	[sib-sam]	102	백이	[pe-ki]
14	십사	[sib-sa]	200	이백	[i-bek]
15	십오	[sib-o]	300	삼백	[sam-bek]
16	십육	[sib-yuk]	400	사백	[sa-bek]
17	십칠	[sib-chil]	500	오백	[o-bek]
18	십팔	[sib-pal]	600	육백	[yuk-bek]
19	십구	[sib-gu]	700	칠백	[chil-bek]
20	이십	[i-sib]	800	팔백	[pal-bek]
21	이십일	[i-sib-il]	900	구백	[ku-bek]
22	이십이	[i-sib-i]	1000	천	[cheon]
23	이십삼	[i-sib-sam]	10000	만	[man]
24	이십사	[i-sib-sa]	100000	십만	[sib-man]
25	이십오	[i-sib-o]	1000000	백만	[peng-man]

Native Korean Numbers

1	하나	[hana]		26	스물여섯	[seu-mul-yeo-seot]
2	둘	[dul]		27	스물일곱	[seu-mul-il-gob]
3	셋	[set]		28	스물여덟	[seu-mul-yeo-deol]
4	넷	[net]		29	스물아홉	[seu-mul-a-hob]
5	다섯	[ta-seot]		30	서른	[seo-reun]
6	여섯	[yeo-seot]		40	마흔	[ma-heun]
7	일곱	[il-gob]		50	쉰	[swin]
8	여덟	[yeo-deol]		60	예순	[yeo-sun]
9	아홉	[a-hob]		70	일흔	[il-heun]
10	열	[yeol]		80	여든	[yeo-deon]
11	열하나	[yeol-hana]		90	아흔	[a-heun]
12	열둘	[yeol-dul]		91	아흔하나	[a-heun-hana]
13	열셋	[yeol-set]		92	아흔둘	[a-heun-dul]
14	열넷	[yeol-net]		93	아흔셋	[a-heun-set]
15	열다섯	[yeol-da-seot]		94	아흔넷	[a-heun-net]
16	열여섯	[yeol-yeo-seot]		95	아흔다섯	[a-heun-ta-seot]
17	열일곱	[yeo-ril-gob]		96	아흔여섯	[a-heun-yeo-seot]
18	열여덟	[yeo-ryeo-deol]		97	아흔일곱	[a-heun-il-gob]
19	열아홉	[yeo-rahob]		98	아흔여덟	[a-heun-yeo-deol]
20	스물	[seu-mul]		99	아흔아홉	[a-heun-a-hob]
21	스물하나	[seu-mul-hana]				
22	스물둘	[seu-mul-dul]				
23	스물셋	[seu-mul-set]				
24	스물넷	[seu-mul-net]				
25	스물다섯	[seu-mul-ta-seot]				

1

첫째 / 첫 번째

[cheot-jje / cheot beon-jje]

first

2

둘째 / 두 번째

[dul-jje / du beon-jje]

second

3

셋째 / 세 번째

[set-jje / se beon-jje]

third

fourth	넷째 / 네 번째	[net-jje / ne beon-jje]
fifth	다섯째 / 다섯 번째	[ta-seot-jje / ta-seot beon-jje]
sixth	여섯째 / 여섯 번째	[yeo-seot-jje / yeo-seot beon-jje]
seventh	일곱째 / 일곱 번째	[il-gop-jje / il-gop beon-jje]
eigth	여덟째 / 여덟 번째	[yeo-teolp-jje / yeo-teolp beon-jje]
ninth	아홉째 / 아홉 번째	[a-hop-jje / a-hop beon-jje]
tenth	열째 / 열 번째	[yeol-jje / yeol beon-jje]

When then?

언제였어요? [eon-je-yeos-seo-yo]

어제
[eo-je]

yesterday

어제저녁
[eo-je-jeo-nyeok]

yesterday evening

그저께
[keu-jeo-gge]

the day before yesterday

지난주
[ji-nan-ju]

last week

작년
[jak-nyeon]

last year

오늘
[o-neul]

today

내일
[ne-il]

tomorrow

모레
[mo-re]

the day after tomorrow

다음주
[da-eum-ju]

next week

내년
[ne-nyeon]

next year

All about time

시간에 관하여 [si-ga-ne gwan-ha-yeo]

시간 [si-gan]	time
시계 [si-gye]	clock
초 [cho]	second(s)
분 [bun]	minute(s)
15분 [sib-o-bun]	quarter of an hour
30분, 반시간 [sam-sib-bun, ban-si-gan]	half an hour
시 [si]	~ o'clock
시간 [si-gan]	~ hour(s) (period of time)

오전

[o-jeon]

morning

정오

[jeong-o]

noon

오후

[o-hu]

afternoon

저녁

[jeo-nyeok]

evening

밤

[bam]

night

자정

[ja-jeong]

midnight

이른
[i-reun]
early

늦은
[neu-jeun]
late

지금 몇 시예요?

[ji-geum myeot si-ye-yo]

What time is it?

7:10 hrs.
오전 **7**시 **10**분이에요.
[o-jeon il-gob si sib bun-i-e-yo]
It's ten past seven a.m.

새벽 1시예요.

[se-byeok han si-ye-yo]

It's one a.m.

7:15 hrs.
오전 7시 15분이에요.
[o-jeon l-gob si sib-o bun-i-e-yo]
It's a quarter past seven a.m.

8: 00 hrs.
오전 8시예요.
[o-jeon yeo-deol si-ye-yo]
It's eight a.m.

9:50 hrs.
오전 9시 50분이에요.
[o-jeon a-hob si o-sib bun-i-e-yo]
It's ten to ten a.m.

10:00 hrs.
오전 10시예요.
[o-jeon yeol si-ye-yo]
It's ten a.m.

10:10 hrs.
오전 10시 10분이에요.
[o-jeon yeol si sib bun-i-e-yo]
It's ten past ten a.m.

10:30 hrs.
오전 10시 반이에요.
[o-jeon yeol si ban-i-e-yo]
It's half past ten a.m.

12:00 hrs.
정오예요.
[jeong-o-ye-yo]
It's midday.

19:55 hrs.
저녁 8시 5분 전이에요.
[jeo-nyeok yeo-deol-si-o-bun jeon-i-e-yo]
It's five to eight p.m.

22:00 hrs.
밤 10시예요.
[bam-yeol-si-ye-yo]
It's ten p.m.

00:00 hrs.
자정이에요.
[ja-jeong-i-e-yo]
It's midnight.

14

Seven days of the week
요일
[yo-il]

월요일	화요일	수요일
[wo-ryo-il]	[hwa-yo-il]	[su-yo-il]
Monday	Tuesday	Wednesday

근무일
[keun-mu-il] work day

주말
[ju-mal] weekend

휴일
[hyu-il] holiday

쉬는 날
[swi-neun nal] day off

목요일	금요일	토요일	일요일
[mo-gyo-il]	[keum-yo-il]	[to-yo-il]	[i-ryo-il]
Thursday	Friday	Saturday	Sunday

오늘은 무슨 요일이에요?   What day is it today?
[o-neu-reun mu-seun yo-il-i-e-yo]

오늘은 월요일이에요.   It's Monday.
[o-neu-reun wol-yo-il-i-e-yo]

오늘은 몇 월 며칠이에요?   What date is it today?
[o-neu-reun myeot wol
myeo-chil-i-e-yo]

오늘은 1월 10일이에요.   It's the 10th of January.
[o-neu-reun il-wol sib-il-i-e-yo]

오늘은 휴일이에요?   Is today a holiday?
[o-neu-reun hyu-il-i-e-yo]

1

일월

[il-wol]

January

2

이월

[i-wol]

February

5

오월

[o-wol]

May

6

유월

[yu-wol]

June

9

구월

[ku-wol]

September

10

시월

[si-wol]

October

The twelve months of the year
열두 달 [yeol-du dal]

3

삼월

[sam-wol]

March

4

사월

[sa-wol]

April

7

칠월

[chil-wol]

July

8

팔월

[pal-wol]

August

11

십일월

[sib-il-wol]

November

12

십이월

[sib-i-wol]

December

The weather and seasons

날씨와 계절 [nal-ssi-wa gye-jeol]

봄

[bom]

spring

여름

[yeo-reum]

summer

가을

[ka-eul]

autumn

겨울

[kyeo-ul]

winter

오늘 날씨가 어때요?
[o-neul nal-ssi-ga eo-tte-yo]

What's the weather like today?

날씨가 좋아요.
[nal-ssi-ga jo-a-yo]

The weather is fine today.

날씨가 화창해요.
[nal-ssi-ga hwa-jang-e-yo]

It's sunny.

날씨가 나빠요.
[nal-ssi-ga na-ppa-yo]

The weather is bad today.

더워요.
[teo-wo-yo]

It's hot.

엄청 더워요.
[eom-cheong teo-wo-yo]

It's very hot.

추워요.
[chu-wo-yo]

It's cold.

엄청 추워요.
[eom-cheong chu-wo-yo]

It's very cold.

바람이 불어요.
[pa-ra-mi bu-reo-yo]

It's windy.

안개가 꼈어요.
[an-ge-ga ggyeo-sseo-yo]

It's foggy.

비가 와요. / 비가 내려요.
[piga wa-yo / piga ne-ryeo-yo]

It's rainy.

이슬비가 와요. / 이슬비가 내려요.
[i-seul-biga wa-yo. /
i-seul-biga ne-ryeo-yo]

It's drizzling.

눈이 와요. / 눈이 내려요.
[nu-ni wa-yo / nu-ni ne-ryeo-yo]

It's snowing.

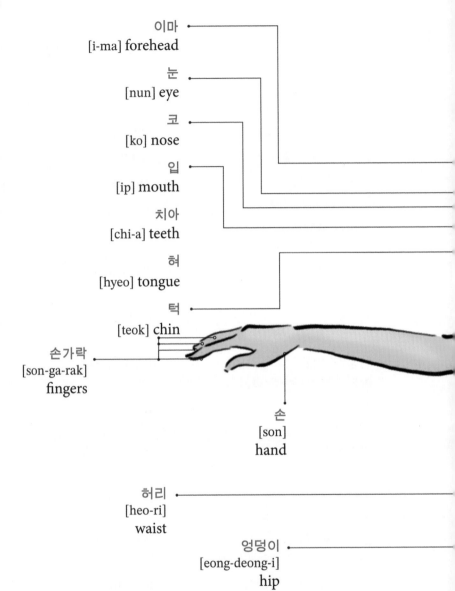

이마
[i-ma] forehead

눈
[nun] eye

코
[ko] nose

입
[ip] mouth

치아
[chi-a] teeth

혀
[hyeo] tongue

턱
[teok] chin

손가락
[son-ga-rak]
fingers

손
[son]
hand

허리
[heo-ri]
waist

엉덩이
[eong-deong-i]
hip

Parts of the body

신체 부위 [sin-che bu-wi]

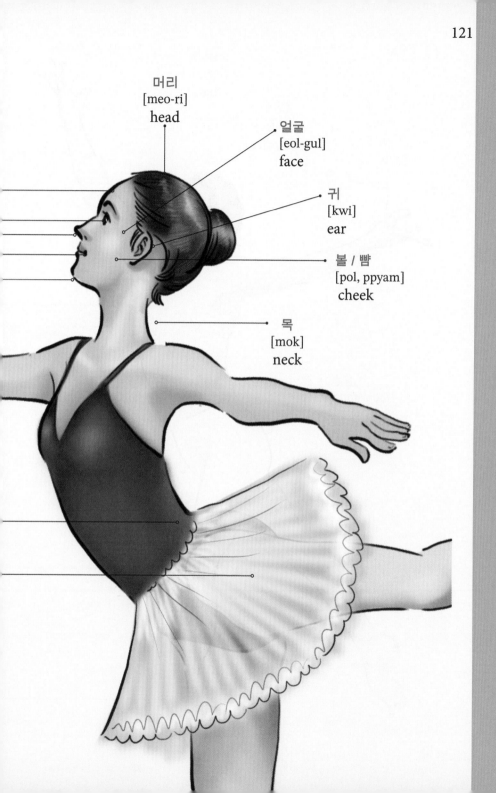

머리
[meo-ri]
head

얼굴
[eol-gul]
face

귀
[kwi]
ear

볼 / 뺨
[pol, ppyam]
cheek

목
[mok]
neck

손
[son]
hand

어깨
[eo-gge]
shoulder

머리
[meo-ri]
hair

등
[deung]
back

몸통
[mom-tong]
body

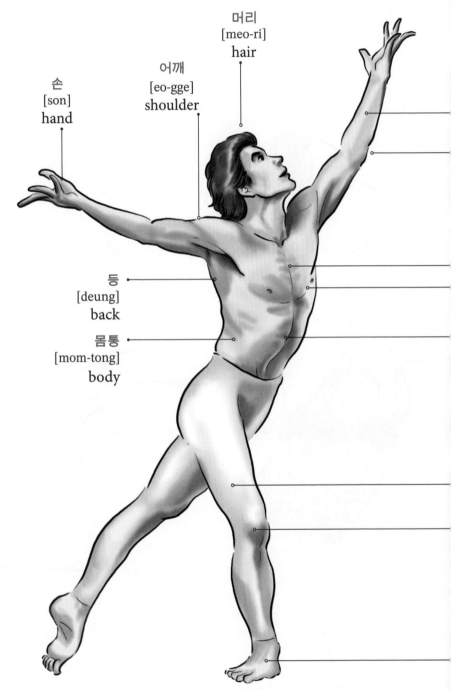

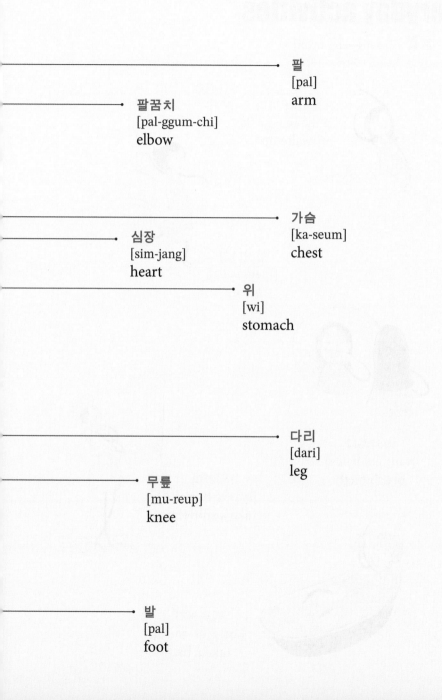

팔
[pal]
arm

팔꿈치
[pal-ggum-chi]
elbow

가슴
[ka-seum]
chest

심장
[sim-jang]
heart

위
[wi]
stomach

다리
[dari]
leg

무릎
[mu-reup]
knee

발
[pal]
foot

Everyday activities

일상 생활 [il-sang seng-hwal]

잠에서 깨다
[ja-me-seo gge-da]
wake up

일어나다
[i-reo-na-da]
get up

양치하다
[yang-chi-ha-da]
brush teeth

샤워하다
[sya-wo-ha-da]
take a shower

목욕하다
[mo-gyok-ha-da]
take a bath

요리하다
[yo-ri-ha-da]
cook

먹다
[meok-tta]
eat

마시다
[ma-si-da]
drink

바라보다
[pa-ra-bo-da]
look at

쓰다
[sseu-da]
write

읽다
[ik-tta]
read

기다리다
[ki-da-ri-da]
wait

만나다
[man-na-da]
meet

주다
[ju-da]
give

기뻐하다
[gi-ppeo-ha-da]
be glad

춤추다
[chum-chu-da]
dance

웃다
[ut-tta]
laugh

울다
[ul-da]
cry

떠나다
[tteo-na-da]
leave

통화하다
[tong-hwa-ha-da]
telephone

운동하다
[un-dong-ha-da]
do sport

그림을 그리다
[keu-ri-meul keu-ri-da]
paint

보다
[po-da]
watch

노래하다
[no-re-ha-da]
sing

사진을 찍다
[sa-ji-neul jjik-tta]
take pictures

놀다
[nol-da]
amuse oneself

사다
[sa-da]
buy

팔다
[pal-da]
sell

일하다
[il-ha-da]
work

배우다
[pe-u-da]
learn

가르치다
[ka-reu-chi-da]
teach

껴안다
[ggyeo-an-da]
hug

사랑하다
[sa-rang-ha-da]
love

키스하다
[ki-seu-ha-da]
kiss

결혼하다
[kyeo-ron-ha-da]
marry

When you feel sick

아플 때 [a-peul-tte]

몸이 안 좋아요. [mo-mi an jo-a-yo]	I don't feel well.
토할 것 같아요. [to-hal geot ga-ta-yo]	I need to vomit.
속이 메스꺼워요. [so-gi me-seu-ggeo-wo-yo]	I feel nauseous.
여기가 아파요. [yeo-gi-ga a-pa-yo]	It hurts here.
열이 있어요. [yeo-ri-is-seo-yo]	I have a fever
머리가 아파요. / 두통이 있어요. [meo-ri-ga-a-pa-yo / du-tong-i is-seo-yo]	I have a headache.
배가 아파요. / 복통이 있어요. [pe-ga-a-pa-yo / bok-tong-i-is-seo-yo]	I have a stomachache.

목이 아파요. [mo-gi-a-pa-yo]	I have a sore throat.
허리가 아파요. [heo-ri-ga-a-pa-yo]	I have backache.
치통이 있어요. [chi-tong-i-is-seo-yo]	I have a toothache.
변비가 있어요. [byeon-biga-is-seo-yo]	I am constipated.
설사를 해요. [seol-sa-reul-he-yo]	I have diarrhea.
알레르기가 있어요. [al-le-leu-giga-is-seo-yo]	I have an allergy.
발진이생겼어요. [pal-jini-seng-gyeos-seo-yo]	I have a rash.

약국
[yak-guk] pharmacy

병원
[byeong-won] hospital

약
[yak] medicine

의사
[ui-sa] doctor

치과의사
[chi-gwa-ui-sa] dentist

검안사
[geom-an-sa] optometrist

간호사
[ka-no-sa] nurse

구급차
[ku-geup-cha] ambulance

괜찮아요?

[kwen-cha-nayo]

Bless you!

Urgency

응급상황 [eung-geub-sang-wang]

화장실이 어디에요?
[hwa-jang-sil-i-eo-di-e-yo]

Where is the toilet?

제가 화장실에 가야 해서요.
[je-ga hwa-jang-sil-e ga-ya he-seo-yo]

I need to go to the toilet.

이 근처에 공중화장실이 있나요?

[i geun-cheo-e gong-jung-wa-jang-sil-i-in-na-yo]

Is there a public toilet near here?

병원에 가야 해요.

[pyeong-wo-ne ka-ya he-yo]

I need to go to the hospital.

도와주세요!　경찰을 불러주세요!

[to-wa-ju-se-yo]　　[kyeong-cha-reul bul-leo-ju-se-yo]

Help!　　　　Call the police, please!

What do these signs mean?

이 표지판에는 뭐라고 쓰여 있을까?

[i pyo-ji-pa-ne-neun mwo-ra-go sseu-yeo i-sseul-gga]

경고

[kyeong-go]

WARNING

진입금지

[jin ip-geum-ji]

NO ENTRY

제한구역

[je-han-ku-yeok]

RESTRICTED AREA

양보

[yang-bo]

YIELD

천천히

[cheon-cheon-hi]

SLOW

버스전용

[peo-seu-jeon-yong]

BUS ONLY

일방통행

[il-bang-to-ngeng]

ONE WAY

주차금지 / 견인지역

[ju-cha-geum-ji / kyeo-nin-ji-yeok]

NO PARKING / TOWING AREA

정지
[jeong-ji]

STOP

노인보호

[no-in-bo-ho]

ELDERLY PROTECTION

어린이보호

[eo-ri-ni-bo-ho]

CHILD PROTECTION

약국

[yak-guk]

PHARMACY

횡단금지

[hoeng-dan-geum-ji]

NO CROSSING

열림

[yeol-lim]

OPEN

닫힘

[ta-chim]

CLOSED

여자화장실

[yeo-ja hwa-jang-sil]

LADIES' RESTROOM

남자화장실

[nam-ja hwa-jang-sil]

MEN'S RESTROOM

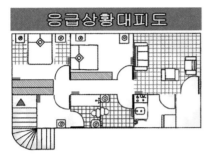

응급상황 대피도
[eung-geub-sang-wang-te-pi-do]

EMERGENCY EVACUATION

비상출구

[pi-sang-chul-gu]

EMERGENCY EXIT

출구

[chul gu]

EXIT

횡단보도

[hoeng-dan-bo-do]

CROSSWALK

자전거횡단

[ja-jeon-geo-hoeng-dan]

BIKE CROSSING

Emotional outbursts

In this chapter we will be dealing with something rather special: emotional outbursts. What, you may ask, does this have to do with a book aimed at introducing a foreign language?

I know that this is quite a sensitive issue and I'm pretty sure that you don't know any other language books that deal with the topic. As I say, I'm inviting you on a risky adventure. But I think it's absolutely essential for you and really useful. I think you need to know this because it can help you to avoid very embarrassing situations when you are in Korea.

First, let me explain what I mean by emotional outbursts. What exactly are they? They are words that simply tumble out of your mouth. You don't usually give them a second thought – they just pop out – and can't be popped back in again, once they're out.

When we are angry, disappointed, afraid, surprised or delighted, we use emotional outbursts to let off steam and regain our calm. We can think of them as turbulence tranquilizers for our emotions.

These outbursts can be more or less violent, depending on intonation and the particular intention or situation in which they are spoken. Gentle outbursts can be mumbled to ourselves to cool our spirits. Violent emotional outbursts are often insulting and deeply hurtful. This type is known in Korean as 욕설 (yog-seol)

So, you can probably now appreciate how difficult and tricky this whole topic is. The fact that I bring up this topic may be unpleasant for the Koreans who are often reserved and polite by nature. However, my intentions are entirely good. I don't want to insult or ridicule their language, but simply to help you avoid making a fool of yourself.

If you hear these Korean words and try to copy them, it's more than likely that you'll get the exact intonation wrong, or it won't come out at quite the right moment, or be appropriate for the person or situation you're in.

So, my first tip is: don't block your ears when you hear them, but don't just copy them either. As a foreigner, you need to get to know them but use them carefully, and only if you're absolutely certain about how and when.

But even if you never use these outbursts yourself, it is certainly helpful to know them. It might avoid a few embarrassing situations or even a slap around the face. This is one of the main reasons for dealing with these phrases.

I hope I've been able to make clear why this topic is an important one in language learning.

Now let's get started:

The first word we will be looking at is the word 씨발 (ssibal)
This word is socially accepted in general usage and frequently heard in Korean drama series. We use the corresponding word in English as well, but it would be impolite to use the direct translation here.

Of course, it's not the literal meaning that is intended when this word is used as an emotional outburst. It is usually used to express anger or frustration with the current situation or with particular person.

Here's a classic example of such a situation: you desperately need to relieve yourself but the only toilet you find is occupied. You can't hold back much longer and in desperation you shout out 씨발 (ssi-bal)

With a bit of luck the current occupant will take note of your desperation and vacate the WC in time.

Here are two Korean emotional outbursts that have roughly the same meaning and differ only minimally from each other. Both are used in similar situations.

The first one is: 제기랄 (je-gi-lal). In English it means: "Damn!". The direct translation saves me from having to explain in which situations it is used.

The second one is 젠장 (jen-jang), which also used to express anger or disappointment.

These two expressions will give you the opportunity to let off steam, and calm down, the same way as "Oh, shit!" in English does.

The expressions we have looked at so far are used mainly in situation when you are alone.The following two words are used when you have company. You can shout this expression at your partner if they have annoyed or disappointed you in any way:

바보 (babo)
멍청이 (meong-cheong-i)

These expressions indicate that the speaker thinks his (or her) partner are not "quite with it". They clearly suggest that the person in question is stupid, has acted stupidly or incorrectly and needs to be told so in no uncertain terms.

The following two expressions convey similar meaning as English emotional outburst: Shut up!

They are 닥쳐 (dag-chyeo) and 입 닥쳐 (ib-dag-chyeo). It is an extremely rude way of making it clear to someone that he or she should be quiet now.

The next two expressions: 미쳤어? (mi-chyeos-seo) and 돌았냐? (do-las- nya)

These emotional outbursts are rather harsh and express a clear annoyance at a person. Either expression will give you the opportunity to speak your mind or communicate your opinion the same way as "Are you crazy?" or: "Are you insane?" in English does.

It gets really fiery when the expression: 개새끼 (ge-se-ggi) is used. When someone uses this expression, they mean that they think the person being abused is the son of a female dog. Of course, this is not to be taken literally, but the injury that results from it is more than clear.

At the very end of the emotional outburst options in Korean:
죽고 싶어? (jug-go sip-peo)
죽을래? (ju-geul-lae)
These two expressions mean "Do you want to die?". Since very few would like to answer this question in the affirmative, one can understand this emotional outburst as a dangerous threatening gesture and it is worth ending the conversation wisely and politely at this point.

Finally, dear readers, let me assure you that I have tried to do all I can to deal with such a sensitive and controversial issue without embarrassing you. I strongly believe that it is important to give you as much confidence as possible when starting to learn the Korean language.

Knowing something about how people express their feelings and emotions is part of that process. I could continue on this theme for some time, but it's enough for you to have a clear idea of the topic, so that you can avoid any embarrassing situations.

Never forget that emotional outburst can vary in meaning as well as in intensity. If you hear one of these phrases, see if you can hear whether the speaker is angry, dissatisfied, furious, or perhaps cracking a joke or making fun of someone.

As far as possible, avoid using these outbursts yourself. Remember, that these words have the power to insult and hurt others and can also be dangerous for you. By using them you are likely to put yourself in a very embarrassing situation, and quite possibly lose face in the process.

브라보!
[peu-ra-bo]

Bravo!

탁월해!
[tak-wol-he]

Excellent!

최고야!
[choe-go-ya]

Super!

완벽해!
[wan-byeo-ge]

Perfect!

Compliments

칭찬 [ching-chan]

훌륭해!
[hul-lyung-he]
Great!

굉장해!
[koeng-ja-nge]
Awesome!

Romance

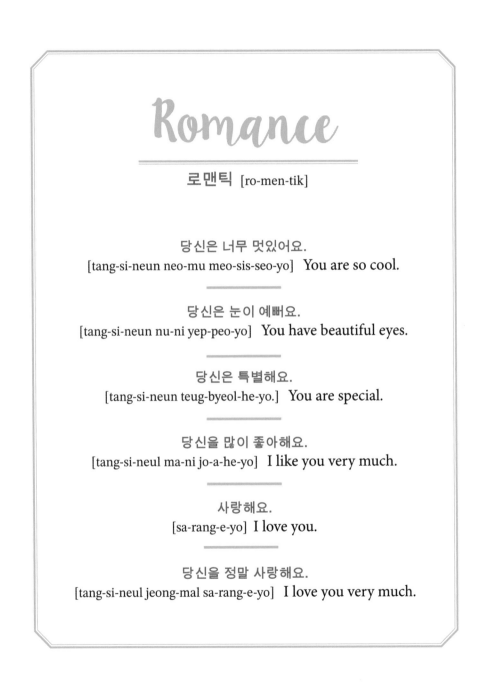

로맨틱 [ro-men-tik]

당신은 너무 멋있어요.
[tang-si-neun neo-mu meo-sis-seo-yo] You are so cool.

당신은 눈이 예뻐요.
[tang-si-neun nu-ni yep-peo-yo] You have beautiful eyes.

당신은 특별해요.
[tang-si-neun teug-byeol-he-yo.] You are special.

당신을 많이 좋아해요.
[tang-si-neul ma-ni jo-a-he-yo] I like you very much.

사랑해요.
[sa-rang-e-yo] I love you.

당신을 정말 사랑해요.
[tang-si-neul jeong-mal sa-rang-e-yo] I love you very much.

당신은 너무 아름다워요.

[tang-si-neun neo-mu a-reum-da-wo-yo]

You are so beautiful.

당신은 멋져요.

[tang-si-neun meot-jyeo-yo]

You are gorgeous.

사랑해.

[sa-rang-e]

I love you.

저와 결혼해 주시겠어요?

[jeo-wa kyeo-ro-ne ju-si-ge-sseo-yo]

Will you marry me?

당신은 너무 예뻐요.

[tang-si-neun neo-mu ye-ppeo-yo]

You are so pretty.

Land and People

땅과 사람들 [ttang-gwa sa-lam-deul]

If you want to learn about the shape and form of Korea, the simplest thing to do is to look at a map. If you want to know more about the people, how they think, how they lead their lives, then the best method is to look at their proverbs. They reveal how the Korean tick.

Often proverbs have developed over centuries as the result of local people's experiences and of the way they think and live their lives. These sayings are passed on from one generation to the next, together with the emotions and moods they convey. Here are a few memorable Korean proverbs:

> 시작이 반이다.
> [si-ja-gi pa-ni-da]
> Beginning is half done.

> 원숭이도 나무에서 떨어진다.
> [won-sung-ido na-mu-e-seo tteo-leo-jin-da]
> Monkeys fall from trees too.
> (Even a master makes mistakes.)

> 소 잃고 외양간 고친다.
> [so il-ko-we-yang-gan ko-chin-da]
> Losing a cow and repairing a barn.
> (Through damage one becomes smart.)

> 세월이 약이다.
> [se-wo-ri-ya-gi-da]
> Time is medicine.
> (Time heals all wounds.)

> 고생 끝에 낙이 온다.
> [ko-seng-ggeu-te-na-g- on-da]
> No pain no gain.

Now you will be able to savor the Korean language like a delicacy. Any worries you may have had about learning this language will turn to joyful confidence.

Korean
at your Fingertips

by
Tien Tammada

Original title: เกาหลีทันใจพูดได้ด้วยปลายนิ้ว เทียร ธรรมดา
© Leelaaphasa.Co.,Ltd.
63/120 Moo 8, Tambon Saothonghin, Bangyai District,
Nonthaburi 11140 Thailand
E-Mail: leelaaphasa2008@gmail.com

1. Edition 2024 (1,01 - 2024)
© PONS Langenscheidt GmbH, Stöckachstraße 11, 70190 Stuttgart, 2024

Translation: Ta Tammadien, Hubert Möller, David Thron
Correction: K. Patanant, Jeonghyun Kim
Cover Design: Leonie Eul
Illustrations Inside: K. Kiattisak, Purmpoon Khamnuanta
Photo Credit Cover: serg_65/Shutterstock, ArtMari/Shutterstock, KUCO/
Shutterstock, YummyBuum/Shutterstock
Typesetting/Layout: Wachana Leuwattananon, Vipoo Lerttasanawanish
Printing and Binding: Multiprint GmbH, Konstinbrod

ISBN 978-3-12-514625-9